THIS BOOK BELONGS TO

....

CROCODILE

PENGUIN

RHINO

ELEPHANT

GIRAFFE

HORSE

BEAR

FROG

SEAL

WOLF

LION

RABBIT

OSTRICH

FOX

SNAKE

PANDA

HIPPO

GOAT

CAMEL

EAGLE

OWL

ZEBRA

BIRD

# MONKEY

DOG
HUSKY

PARROT

TIGER

WALRUS

DEER

RAM

LEMUR

MEERKAT

SQUIRREL

CHEETAH

# RED PANDA

FAWN

PIG

DOLPHIN

DOG
DALMATIAN

WHALE

FISH

BUNNY

CROCODILE

SHEEP

OWL

# HIPPO

HEDGEHOG

SNAKE
COBRA

BULL

EAGLE

FROG
ON BRANCHE

PANDA ON A TREE

BEAR

SQUIRREL

TIGER

APE

OWL

MONKEY

ELEPHANT

PENGUIN